Matches Strike Boxes

poems by

Jane Spencer

Finishing Line Press
Georgetown, Kentucky

Matches Strike Boxes

ACKNOWLEDGMENTS

The Power of the Feminine "I": Leaves dress me now
Moss Puppy: Indian Point, When Crickets Sing
Portland Press Herald: If the universe was a bar; Sonar
Halcyone/Black Mountain: Burning Violin
Haunted Waters Press: Hive
HummingbirdPress: Fish Market
HummingbirdPress: Sparking Stars
Linden Ave Lit.com: At the End of the Day

Publisher: Leah Huete de Maines
Editor: Christen Kincaid
Cover Art: Jane Spencer
Author: Photo: Jane Spencer
Cover Design: Elizabeth Maines McCleavy

Order online: www.finishinglinepress.com
also available on amazon.com

Author inquiries and mail orders:
Finishing Line Press
PO Box 1626
Georgetown, Kentucky 40324
USA

Contents

For Lee, my love

In the Clock Box
After M. Jean Craig

What do you feed him?

Baby dragons don't eat.

How will you feed him when he gets stronger?

I won't need to.

How will he breathe with the seams taped?

No need for air yet.
It just needs to be warm and quiet.
Until it's hatched.

Make the hole bigger.

No. Soft wings need dark.

May I see him?

No. He's too shy. He's about to hatch.

When will that be?

When it's ready.

How will you know?

When I can keep my marbles in it again.

Field Day

Standing in a pasture of brown cows,
the silk of their milk in their velvet udders.
I touch with my small hand,
the cow, placid-eyed,
glances back.

Crouching under barbed wire, I lift my legs over
into the tall grasses, wildflowers,
piles of muck
where a bull sports
a magnificent hump between his shoulders.

Mother calls, her steps,
great strides away into another uneven field.

The honey smell of sun—
the bull watching me—
A spreading of farms and intersecting fences,
humming summer day—

He snorts, kicks back a hoof's worth of dirt,
then waits.

I turn to run freely down a nearby hill,
feel the heated air rush at my puffy smock dress,
bare legs, arms, muddy tennis shoes,
pixie brown hair.
Lie on our picnic cloth, sure to be visited by wasps, bees,
ants.
Watch their clumsy navigating
sticky paper wrappings, crumbs of sandwiches.
Topographical challenges: furrows and puckers of cloth.

We are already in the afterlife.
At least, I am.

Aging evolved into a strength.
Life, dreamy.
We've learned so much about what not
to do. And letting the unexpected take
its course—

ingrained. Death: ironclad as a bank vault.
Nowhere near it.
Seeing favorite friends,
laughing, celebrating any size event of the day,
making light of nuisances and peculiarities. Dividing
experiences between
problems versus expenses.
Having time, I'm definitely past dying. This is just too good.

I must've skipped it.
Crossed a bridge, but there was no touching.
Had to have been the Hudson, my childhood favorite.

I can't have swum, since I broke my hip,
but one night, those towers did slide by me,
as sharply as seeing around corners.
Magnificent reach of cables and arches upward,
an ethereal ink line drawing made solid. I was relieved
I'd felt her strength pulling me close again.
If I'd attempted to traverse on the top lanes,
I'd have been cradled,
as if lifted, nestled in a suspended wire net.

Could you wear

python heels, comfortably?
Wouldn't they feel constricting—-overly muscular?
Stealthy—slick?
Crushing-bones.

Paralyzing you— like prey?

If the Universe was a bar,

what would they serve?
My favorite girlfriend, Tori,
game for about anything,
took a violet drink, sat
at the counter, and then exalted in the
taste of lavender, macaroons, the smell of
powdery romance. And the crystal-faceted ice cubes,
beneath lush petals floating near the rim.
Men love her, the bartender wearing
a sequin of stars in his pointed man-bun,
made sure to link his sparkling eyes on hers, often.
I'm not into changing my drink,
and received my usual.
Vodka, corrosive as sleet.
Rocks dirty, spitting grit between my teeth,
live clams squirting sand.

Tori's such a looker, currently engaging
 with the women in white to her other side,
who says, *It's not as if anyone who visited Hades ever got a
return ticket!*

And—
the despondent guy beside her says, *if that
was God he would, and he'd better damn well return
to say he was sorry.*

All the stools stood empty as a row of soldiers, asleep on
their feet. If I sat there long enough,
how long till they close?
Doors locked, purple cursive lights against the window, dimmed.
Policemen's flashlights swung their blazes inward,
a den of pool tables, dirty linoleum squares, moving on
without eyes following them.

Various Songs of the Northern Mockingbird

Among the everglades,
the only spiraling thing:
the neck of the python.

I was of three minds,
as on a mangrove tree
dangled three pythons.

The python whirled in the brushfires:
a small dance of knowledge.

A man and a woman
are one.
A man and a woman and a python
are one less.

I do not know which to prefer,
the beauty of inflection
or innuendos.
The python gulping a palm rat
Or just after.

Humidity filled the long window
with blurry glass.
The shadow of the python
crossed it, to and fro.
The mood
traced in the shadow
an unravelling effect.

Small mammals have vanished;
the python will snack on
small children, legs at the edge of a pool.

Pythons rarely seen:
watch anyone from up in trees,
rocky openings.

At the sight of pythons
dispersing as if green light
rays, movement is harmonious.

The river is moving.
The python too.

It was evening all afternoon.
It was pouring
and was going to thunder.
The pythons coiled
in the river's cool mud.

Light in the Sky

Between sky and water,
a glow holds its own reflection.
Tints air lavender, soaks water purple.

Better than a theatre's stage,
cloaked by colored lights,
but surrounded just the same as
with dark, velvety curtains.

Shoreline's blackness
deep as smeared charcoal—
layer upon layer,
pressed into soft paper.

Beauty is best—after sun has left.
A lens cannot capture it.
The sky, a clear bowl of
delicate washed color,
blended,
and spun—rapidly—

by night.

If on a winter's night a traveler

struggles through deepening snow,
tilting against the wind,
boot-printing letters into the
hills
followed by the shadows of tall, thin, men in stovepipe hats
leaning far ahead of themselves, down into
valleys
whispering as they
snatch each letter,
stash inside their topcoats.

Relishing vowels,
perfect snowflakes.
Their legs lope and yank,
as if drawn quickly by pulleys.

Having reached their needed twenty-five,
they run, tail coats flapping behind
past mice, crows, shivering—

The early beets of May

Whiten the porcelain
baking dish,
your magenta orbs, doubly radiant,
in water, gleaming.

I'm not accustomed to so much light.

And, new life, tiny, and sweet.
Arriving when I'm exhausted
of dumpy squash, potatoes and onions.
When a blue sky shocks me, as if the
pigeon grey curtain drew itself
open, to what had
always been present, in waiting.

Rubbing your slippery skin off, I'm
starving. Your velvety taste
lingers on my tongue. The taste of earth without grit.

You let me feel the weight of a color,
burgundy-purple. Soon I wear
your gorgeous shade,
fingers and palms stained.
My nipple rings as dark violet as yours.

Mauve-crimson chunks, trickling
pigmented creeks across a white plate. Your pure plainness
must be honored
by a simple steam!

Blinding

sun bouncing off a silver sea
rain falls unexpectedly
while this day
still has sun to spill

Blinding white as an
arc welders light. Their eyes
covered by dark glass.
Their finger-size torches melting,
metal pools, merging gaps into solid
seams.

Then suddenly, the shower shifts
back into the sky

as if
to say

I wasn't
here,
you just
dreamed
my drops

believing them
tossed

carelessly.

In daydreaming

I put the world away, allow,
a rich source of sparks
and spontaneity between
sleep and wakefulness.

Nothing to do with immortality.
I would want this process often.

But why, always a ferry man?
Why not my bleach blonde
Labrador who'd
gently hop onto the banks
of the river of death,
shaking it off as spray,
grinning with rubber lips
as if I were love's
playful spirit? Who glides with me
astride her spine: she wants me
to feel water's ease. And
my whole body spreads wide
as the overhead elm's
reflected leaves up and down the tributary,
as the wind flutters,
through her fur, flipping over the corners
of my new body.
Easy to pull me, flattened,
between her teeth, to the sunny field—
we'd rush above the river,
lay out to dry.

Some vines twine,

some won't.
Some swing out from
trellises, pricking the
atmosphere. Others
wait to be captured,
suckered by their companions.

Earlier, open leaves learnt
to hold a shape without labor. Now,
some curl inward,
preferring to cling, loop
tangle. Exist in
the thick of it. Fly fish
their tips around one another's stem
for support. Enjoy threading
the needle.

Others latch fast,
to a single point
considering that enough.
Some let effort slip,
or wait so long to decide
they end up crushed to the rear.

The
knotting kind, they call themselves.

Tightly knit.

When we are in conversation,

When we are in conversation,
another call eclipses our connection.

When I've finally surrendered to the meandering
mind, a dinging cuts off the flow.

When I give in to check,
I detach myself from an interesting depth, a richer
supply of oxygen.

Turning it all off is the only way to part.
Like getting up deliciously early,
The new day not yet begun, in
that gap
between the prior day
and the present,
the house belongs to you.

Once, put last, repeatedly on a walk,
I quit a potential friendship.
Too rude, the one-way conversation,
I'm just saying after each comment.
Not listening to any voice but her own.

Snowy—

Punk rock queen.
Velvet blue legs,
pointed tip boots,
shaggy white coat
topped off by pink protruding lips,
black tip.
Could you have been a starlet,
not a sinuous egret
grazing a still pond?
Gliding up a dark
corridor of shiny glass,
between rushes of camera bulbs flashing
round and round your one watchful eye.

Salty water laps tiny taps

against rocks
along our shore. Slipping
up

sliding back

tap, lap slap pat.

Rhythmic assertions

blending with a breeze

traipsing leisurely

through a screen at the
back

of the house

out the open front door,

tingling over my bare legs,

sweat drying cool—
I'm transfixed. My skin
softening.

Unable to think. Amazed
at the texture of the sounds,
breeze
flowing right through me.
I am being breathed.

Vinegar

Rotten,
mushy and sour,
at the base of a scrawny
tree.

I stink of vinegar,
unfit for jelly or pie.

Fuzz of mildew greyed over,
crows regard me as stone.
Worms wiggle the long way around.
Maggots too picky,
their refuge,
firmer flesh.

My skin wrinkled, loose,
bruised.
Shrunken,
I no longer have form.

Absorb this soul, soil.
Please, put me to use.
Feeding the tree, next
year's fruit,
sweating—
tart,
juice.

Teardrop from the Gods

Knife drives into muscles,
valves grip tight.
The turn, tear of blade
under flesh,
sand scrapes against bone,
shells spread open,
glossy china rims,
blue milk cups.
Tip one onto my tongue.
Oh! Glorious body,
you're mine.

Every time I weed my circular garden,

I turn the two chairs at center
toward each other. When I turn back,
at sunset, I imagine a terrific woman
has come and gone.
Someone curious to listen to,
lively and unpredictable. Whom
I want to know more about.
Who's been content to linger,
take in the day,
make me laugh.

You see how the chairs just
inched closer? Their heads must've
leaned in. They found they have a bond:
we like the same kind of women. No fuss.

One day, it seemed they were two silent islands.
What fearful thing could be amiss?
Don't be deceived. Plenty of acceptance
equals no need to say anything.

Chair arms rated, next to each other
the friends could have
shifted to greet the angle of sun-toasting
skin between trees.
Fingers, stoking the coolness of grass.

Leaves dress me now:

spring jacket
blaring emerald skirt.

Spurt forth, your
clapping hands,

fluttering fringe,
hide those motionless forked sticks.

Shake, swivel, slip,
flag and wave behind
and beside our houses,
spread through the forest.

Sweep brushing sounds
through air. Catch on
oaks like streamers.

Give rain a surface to patter
upon. Smear the landscape,

a rich green blur. Knit complicated
patterns across grass,

paths, woodlands, gardens.
Grow and shrink shadows, in slow

motion. Open—
settle in. I'll finish by dispersing flowers.

Strips of Sunlight

appear over the empty steamer chair
in my sunken garden.
A slim glow, along a single
wooden arm,
down the leg rests' slopes,
a shadowy slide,
serviceberries—
the mass of a weary
maple, bending
over—a single moan
inside her crusted
trunk, as growth rings
strain to compress over
themselves. My breath, sounding
held under water. Traced in light, such
elegance collapses completely
as night falls—

A glass of water

holds tiny cupping apricot blossoms
able only to sip water,
and sun
as a person sips
espresso.

Did they evolve like that—so delicate, and fine--
in order to have less to lose?
Rosy threads of feathery antennae inside
star-shape bracts, seem
barely capable of procreating,
yet more grow each year.

Did surviving unpredicted spring
cold snaps
make them cautious. And
what about me? Did the chill
ready me to protect them?
Dashing out with my scissors,
I wanted to save them from giving up.

They show us resilience, patience,
amidst our rush-to-finish world.
Are you, dear blooms, better off in a vase then wasting
a year's preparation
blown,
shredded,
wind-scattered
across plain grass?

On our kitchen table, soft sun streaming
through their translucent petals,
simple as newborn skin.

Do I want to open my eyes

Do I want to open my eyes
see the time?
No.

Nose nuzzled in the pillow,
I'm not moving a limb,
I want stillness, pure
stillness, like everything around me.

Nothing audible—
except one sparrow's chipping call.
This is grounding, which I rarely feel.

A stick ticks against a roof shingle.

So pleasant. Undemanding sound.
But the moment is moving.
Beyond my eyelids,
I feel the room lighten, widen.

My mind is a murky strip of smog. Wanting
brightness, I
open my eyes slowly.

Drink patiently, as a monk's one cup of the day.
Last night's dream lingering at the bottom.

—I'd like to die with my friends at a table,

—I'd like to die with my friends at a table,
 just before the end of a raucous laugh.
One that torques me forward, or
throws arching back, gasping, heart
swelling, toes squeezing, eyes streaming,
head reeling, at how fantastically outrageous a
comment or joke was. The moment
when, a laugh's with us, on us, and
we are, in that tingling, sheer moment of
rising, to hold onto what we made together a
tiny second more.

That way, I'll avoid the weepy
slowing down, when
we regain our posture, and
switch to water.
When—
the reality of where we
really are,
seeps back in.

Like the whales

Like the whales, I emerged from the sea.
I'm my most dreamy underwater,

though not as fluid as those
who tried living on land,
growing four legs from fins,

turning around, retracting their landing
gear, returning to the ocean.

That was when the first humans arrived.
Bringing the establishment of ownership,
greed, and waste.

I don't believe the scientists' answer: food supply
was more plentiful in the ocean. They had to have known.

My animal instinct tells me, whales have enormous
clairvoyant powers, extending their
echolocation far out into the future, as a sounding
device—now here.
If they knew then,
nothing for living would remain,
perhaps we should be asking them now:
where to go next,
and what to ask of the body.

Sonar

Dark October,
hovering over sourdough, soft butter, figs—
hot black tea. Graced by a
majestic undertow,
cello diving on the radio.
Plates of thinly-vinegared leaves,
miniscule sprouts,
revive
while a booming ocean
slopes into the shoreline—
impossible to see.

Indian Point

Glowing with late autumn's sun,
a few remaining monarchs and
the warty pods of milkweeds,
spilling out silky-tufted parachutes,
flat brown seeds,
wind-riding passengers.

The ground's bland damp, splattered by
discarded nut shells,
acorn berets, burrs, red berries—

A few pop-up mushrooms,
shaped like tongues, parasols,
ears laid atop others, married to dead trees.
The gills underneath their heads:
folded pleats.
As quickly as they come,
barely settle in,
they vanish.

November's days,
diminished light, muted
color—locks up every smell.

A tiny world, in the flooded ditches

of December.
Collections of apple red, burgundy, golden brown
showing off under a glossy roof of magnifying ice.
A museum case unfurling at my feet.

When our blood
slows to the local speed
appreciation serves us the most.
It's icy, but there's sun.
The screams from wind, horrible, but roads are safe.
The snow may not have left, but generously reflects
sun. Melts for growth underground,
for a yield appearing later.
And fires help us forget.

I worship the splendid, burning smells:
cherry, oak, and pine. Sweet, succulent.
Perhaps, bacon too, laced with
pipe smoke. Lively sounds crack,
snap, collapse, re-arrange, resettle, inside
the fire box.

In better states of the year,
the trees' missing colors
reproduced by flame:
shimmery oranges, blazing golds, and unique
patterns in partly-devoured wood. Burnt
longer, chinks of geometric
squares divide up a glowing log, gorgeous guts
spilling out, rimmed in sheaths of
black, shouldered by silvery ash.

"Lovely Evening"

My parents had elegant parties.
Dapper-dressed men
in sassy eyeglasses,
freshly shaved and patted cheeks.
Confident women, smartly-cut clothes.
lavish shoes—
metal ice shakers
rattle clink.

Gold hoop earrings flashed in candlelight.
Mirrored platters swirled round--
tables strewn with cocktail napkins,
clear buckets of melting ice,
salty cashews, I was allowed to serve.

By dark, group voices crescendo.
Matches strike boxes,
cigarettes glowed,
as they settled into silver-tongued voices.
I was directed off to bed.

With Thanks

I am grateful to the many people who have supported the creation of this manuscript. Rebecca Givens-Rolland, poet and teacher, for teaching me how to say so much with so few words, setting me on a delicious path. To my husband, Lee, for his faith in my abilities. My dear friends: Tori and Gary Rubin, Gri and Phil Font-Mason, Bj and David Williams, for their reading support. My siblings Helen, Sarah, and David for their applause. My mother, for turning me onto books from an early age, and feeding my hunger through high school. My sculptor father for training my eye. And my children, Mark and Lesley, having lovingly tolerated my infatuation with art for a long time.

After working in the fine arts for decades, Jane Spencer switched to poetry. She loves expressing visual images in words, pulling meaning from the natural world, and contemplating our place within it. The pandemic turned her focus on how we think about death, vaccination led her to the afterlife.

Jane says poems allow her to connect unrelated experiences. A wonderful process of surprise and discovery for the soul.

www.ingramcontent.com/pod-product-compliance
Lightning Source LLC
Chambersburg PA
CBHW022052080426
42734CB00009B/1317